What is America?

ISBN 978-1-7343004-1-3

Copyright © 2020 Carolyn Lewis

God's Creations Publishing Inc.
PO Box 417
Mexico, MO 65265
godscreationpub@yahoo.com

All rights reserved. No part of this publication may be reproduced, stored in a retreival sstem, or transmitted in any way by any means – electronic, mechanical, photocopy, recording or otherwise – without the prior permission of the copyright holder, except as provided by USA copyright law.

Cover & Layout Design by Holly Hyde
Posy Creative
posycreative.com

Scripture quotations are taken from:
THE HOLY BIBLE, NEW INTERNATIONAL VERSION®, NIV®
Copyright © 1973, 1978, 1984, 2011 by Biblica, Inc.™
Used by permission. All rights reserved worldwide.

Finally, all of you, have *unity* of mind, sympathy, brotherly *love*, a tender heart, and a *humble* mind.

1 Peter 3:8

Do nothing from rivalry or conceit but in *humility* count *others* more significant than *yourselves*.

Philippians 2:3

TABLE OF *Contents*

America	5
Them, They, Us	13
Poverty	19
Too Much	25
Nothing Just Happens	33
Be Accounted For	39
Free	47
35 Days	55
Democracy	63
Stories Unknown	69
Hamlett	77
Bipartisan	85
Impeachment	93
Real People	103
Along the Way	111
The American Dream	118
Ways to Donate	120

What does America stand for? Is America the people, or is America the people it represents? This is the question being presented daily. Is anyone listening? Does anyone care?

Are the majority of American people being heard? Does it even matter anymore? Has America just become those, them and these? How about we? Ask yourself this: what does America mean to you, and are you happy with your view?

America

America – whose America?
For what, America?
And
For whom?
America, home of the brave
Brave enough to face
Not being shot in school
Brave enough to work
Yet, being willing to choose food over being rude
America, land of the free
Free to die
Free to be working poor
Free to know that my rights
Matter not to 'tis of thee
Let mortal tongues awaken
From settling for less and needing and need no more
Let all that breathe partake
And not be counted out

(cont.)

Yet, In
And, say to what America truly stands for
Let rocks their silence break
The spirits of people unwilling
To acknowledge we are all
Living
Breathing
Human beings
Needing
Wanting
And worth much more
Let not America be a wasteland of death
To anything but wealth
Let America stand for something
Much greater than
The just "Me" yet the "We"
And much more

"In God We Trust." Do we?

NOTES

NOTES

Notes

Notes

Justice may be *Blind*, but are we? Do we not see that fair does not have a *Universal* meaning to 'tis of thee? Does not the word *We* include you, me, them, they, us? Or does it just imply that you are not me?

— Carolyn Lewis

Them, GOVERNMENT
They, Us
5%   WE THE PEOPLE

They say we are different from Them
Because
They are not one of us
They don't like Them
Because
Them look too much like Us
They are apart of the Them
That
Does not want to become Us
They are the Them
That
Created Us
Who are they to tell
Them
Not to hear us
One day the Us
will empower the Them
And
They will know
how We the people feel
And
Then we will be heard

WHAT IS AMERICA? | 13

Notes

Notes

Notes

Notes

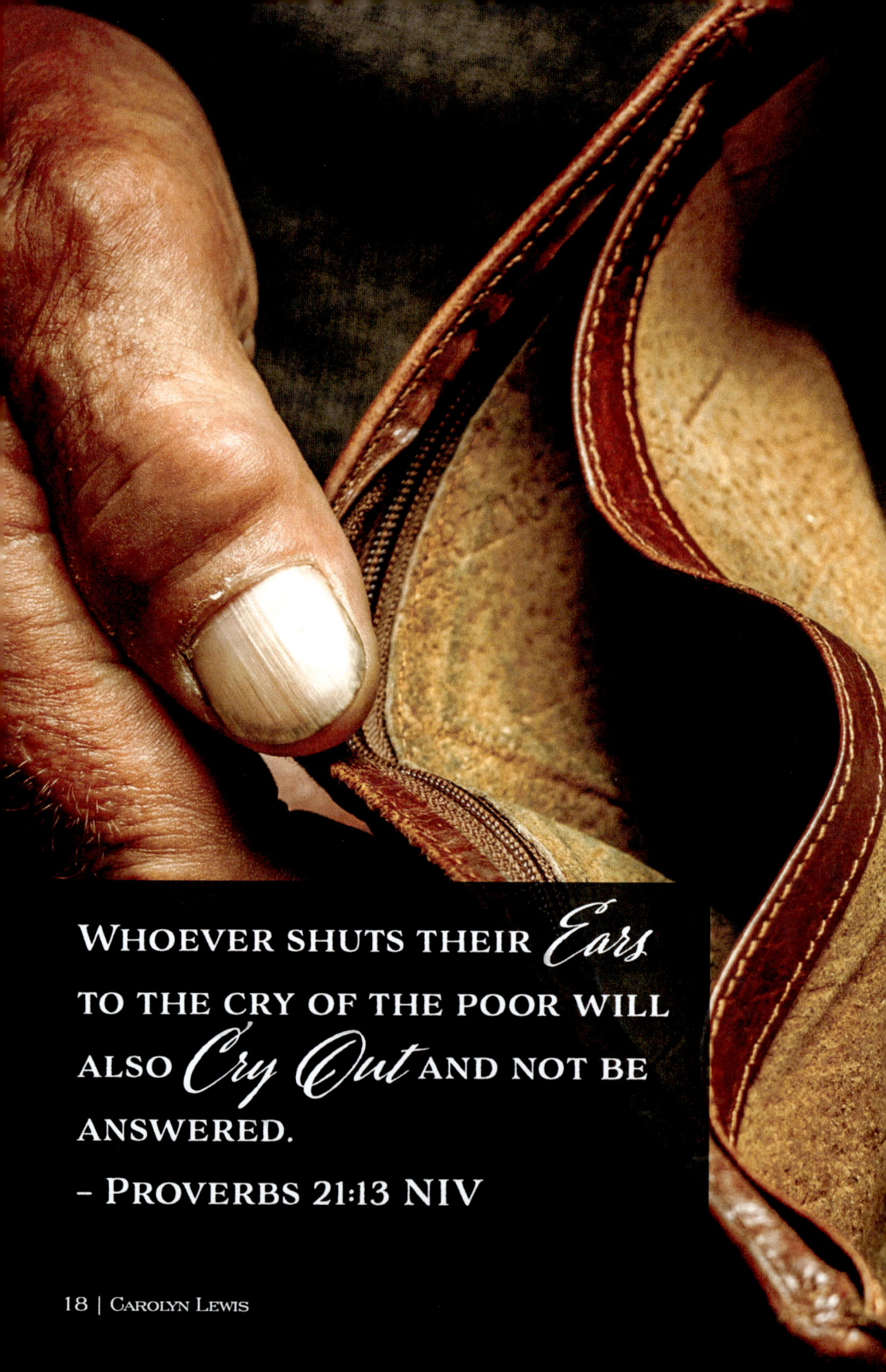

Poverty

Poor, lacking, having less than
Overlooked, undervalued and outweighed
Variety of people, grossly out of proportion and not expected to succeed
Economically rarely exposed or given access to successful opportunities
Ratio of people far beyond what is believed
Targeted amount that far outweighs just simple greed
Yearning for things, you're not sure you even believe

Poor, overlooked variety of an economical ratio of targeted people, yearning for real access to opportunities to prosper.

This is what poverty means.

Notes

Notes

Notes

Notes

Too Much

Too much of this
Too much of that
Too much
Too much fat
Too much work
Too much wack
Too much
Too much love
Too much sex
Too much touch
What's up with that
Too many choices
Too many facts
Too many which one is that
Too much
When does too much develop into hoarding
Hoarding is brought on by a trauma

(cont.)

A trauma that causes this reaction
Too many people are hoarding
Too many people are going through a trauma
And
No one is developing a show to help spotlight
So
Others can be entertained by their suffering
To only watch and truly be able to relate
Reality television shows
Reality Presidents
Reality Entertainment
Real or Entertainment
Which is it
And
What does it say about America

Notes

Notes

Notes

Notes

NOTHING JUST

Truth
What happens is what we know
Truth
Will the truth make us grow
Truth
Will we accept what we know
Truth
Will we allow ourselves to acknowledge
What we know, so we can grow
Truth
Is what we see all that we know
No! No! No!
Truth
It will fester and grow
Because
God will always let us know
Truth
Secrets can't hide the truth
Dirty little lies
We believe to be unknown
Things we tell ourselves to believe
Are unknown only to be seen

Notes

Notes

Notes

Notes

Be Accounted For

It's not going to work if all we do is Follow

We must create what we want for our Tomorrows

Living in the shadows just won't do

And

We just can't continue to hope our way through

Fight, Speak, Stand up

And

Be accounted for

Because this is just as much about you as me

We may not be neighbors

Or

Even closely in a comparison view

Yet one thing is true

That I need you and you need me

Even if, only from a view

What are you waiting for?

Do you not want to

Be accounted for

(cont.)

Unknown
Unseen
Unheard
That is what sounds absurd
If not NOW, then when
is not
Everything
Something
Anything
Worth fighting for
Don't you want to have a say
Or
Would you rather leave this world in a disarray
Because leave we must
But
How we can choose
Is nothing worth fighting for?
Does it not matter to you at all?

Notes

Notes

Notes

NOTES

> CONFORMITY IS THE *jailer* OF FREEDOM AND THE ENEMY OF GROWTH.
> — JOHN F KENNDY

Free

Is anything really free
Free will
Will to do what?
With whom
Or even for whom
Freedom of speech
To whom
When
Where
And How
Arrest records would lead to a different opinion
Inciting a riot, disturbing the peace, interfering in an
active investigation, interfering with the
law – just to name a few
There can be no spin placed on a case without a lawyer
appointed to win, only a settlement of
justice that was never meant to have a win,
this is the result of too many people's end

(cont.)

Freedom to choose
Says who
Where does that happen
And how much is ever enough
When will the world be blind enough to no longer be able to see
Oh and no longer able to hear, because you know
We know what ethnicity sounds like, right
Asked the richest persons of different ethnicities their experiences of freedom to choose and see
if the barriers differ
Being looked down on by a person, when you have no money is the status quo as opposed to
being looked down upon with an endless amount of monies somehow seems insulting – why?

Freedom of religion
Everyone has a cross to bear
You can't get a divorce, have sex outside of marriage

You have to repent
Etc., and so on. . .
Freedom to love
How many times have you loved a person that did not
even love themselves
How many children have killed their parents
How many parents have killed their children
Domestic violence
Stalking
F – Familiar
R – Reasoning
E – Explaining
E – Extemporaneous reactions
Because if we truly explored these freedoms
we would not come to the definition of free
meaning without compensation. Let's stop using the word
out of context when it suits our cause
and deal with the reality of the true meaning daily to
make real life long changes.
You can't make real change if you are not using real words.

Notes

Notes

Notes

Notes

35 Days

35 days that felt like an eternity

35 days with much despair

35 days without a here nor there

35 Days…………

Are they even aware

35 Days without a day to be aware

35 days with no end in sight

35 days with nothing but the plight

35 Days…………..

35 days to realize we don't matter in this fight

35 days to realize we did not cause this strife

35 days could end a life

35 Days…………..

35 days went on much too long

35 days is how long it took America to be reborn

35 days should not be the end

35 days should show America we must become Greater

(cont.)

from within
35 Days…………..
35 days did not make America great again
35 days made America weaker from within
35 days made Americans analyze their dismay
35 Days………….
Will America be able to survive another 35 days
Will America make changes, that caused such a disarray
Will America grow to her full potential
Or
Will America falter and crumble as if
without any potential

Notes

Notes

Notes

Notes

Nearly all men can stand *Adversity* but if you want to test a man's *Character*, give him power.

– Abraham Lincoln

Democracy

D emonstrates the ability to
E nable actions through
M ovement of the people by the people within the United States
O f America with a
C reditable system that is
R eliable and that demonstrates
A ccurate facts through
C ommunication with and for the people
Y earning for a cohesive change by one for all

Based not on a class, gender or ethnicity, yet governed only by the Constitution of the United States of America, governed by no one man alone yet by "We the People" through democracy for the people. This is when democracy will represent the people who are most affected by it.

Notes

Notes

Notes

Notes

STORIES
Unknown

Everyone has their own story of poverty

In their own version

Known and unknown

Someone who has had to reach

beyond where they have now grown

To be able

To teach knowledge

To lead people

Even yourselves

To where you are currently at or stride to be

This

Is a story that can not only be left up to me

We must all understand that our stories are important

enough to share

(cont.)

Not out of
Shame
Embassrament
Judgment
or
Guilt
Yet out of
Knowledge
Power
Growth
Prosperity
And most of all because we all need to know
We are created equally, no matter our economic status
We all struggle
Different choices lead to different solutions
My struggles, not yours and yours, not mine
yet we all have struggled

Notes

Notes

Notes

NOTES

Hamlett

Judge L. R. Hamlett
To be judged with no cause
Not at all
I did not put you here
I was neither there nor anywhere, near
What just cause brought you here
Not me at all
This was you
Who seen this through
To have caused you to be near
If it was you, who did whatever they say you did
I am here to hear your plea
Legally and fairly
So don't get too snooty
Because it is within my duties

(cont.)

To demand and receive respect
Which I also have been giving
Yes, I am here to carry out the laws of the land
Yet
I am always willing to lend a hand to fellow man
When and if I can
If the circumstances will allow
Allow yourselves to see mercy and grace does dwell
Within sight
In spite of why you stand before me
You stand before me for the law to judge
circumstance as the law requires
I am not the one who has your final say
So, remember to always obey
So, not to view this as the only way

Notes

NOTES

Notes

Notes

Bipartisan

You were not born me
And
Me not you
So, what does that bring me to do
Should I want to be you
Only
To be afforded a better view
Or
Should I just wait for a better view, of what it is, you do?
Should I want or deserve
What is due you
Or
Due me
Should there be a difference for me
As opposed to you
I female
You male
What are we to do
Examine, evaluate, measure
What I am, to you, or you to me

(cont.)

Everyone matt

Is such an examination even possible
If I, alone am me
And
You alone are you
Female and male,
Is that not
What we are meant to be
There is no other than He or she
So together
We represent
We
We the people are what we are said to be
Or
Is this a representation
Of what is "to be"?
I don't want a world that just represents me
Nor
Do I want a world that I can not see
I want to see a world that evolves me
As much as you
That we both could see
A world where we can accept one another as a
Me being me and you being you
No matter male or female
That's a view that represents a "we"

Notes

Notes

Notes

Notes

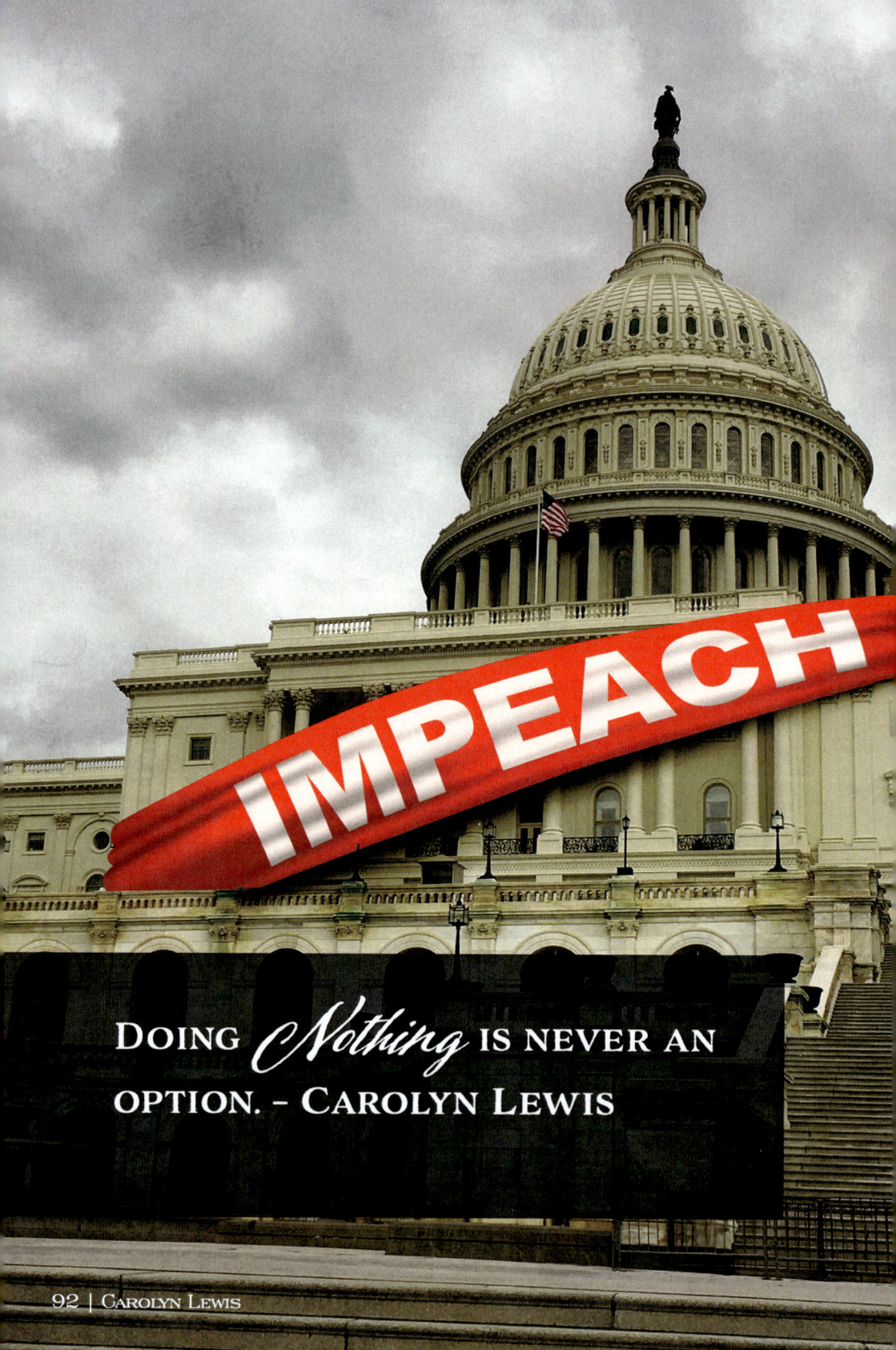

Impeachment

The United States has been impeached
Impeached by the American people
Not by the House of Representatives
Nor
By Senate or Congress
Yet
The United States Citizens of America
Founded for the people by the people
Or
Wait, was it or are we
The founded people are who
Not
Me
Nor
You
Then who
Did we create the America we see
Or
Did Democracy do this to me

(cont.)

The democracy that I, as the people feel

Fully

And

Wholly represents Me

My rights have been changed to meet none of my needs

My rights have been changed to want, forever more

My rights have been changed to no one hears my cry

Not even an uttered word will be spoken of nor for

Why

Because there is no love

Love for Humanity

Love for one another

Love for Brother or Sister

Nothing seems to matter at all

Nothing

No one

No place, person or thing

Yet

Wait – does it

That almighty dollar

Always seems to win the day

It tells people
Who to listen to
Who's important and who's not
Who to use
Who is able to be abused
Who matters and who matters not at all
We can not keep falling victim to this sin
Even the ones that are the victims of this often sin too,
from within
Reality shows, watching and imitating, as to relate
Magazines and opinions of people we don't even know
You matter not because you are not from my hood
You know them! They probably were!
That's what they get for!
Shouldn't "all lives matter"?
If we want to be truly inclusive
A "movement" is just that, an idea, a thought, a challenge,
that is about changing one thing to another
The question is, is moving from one thing to another
thing, better if it is not the right thing?
Vote you say!

(cont.)

Then you will win!
Win what, I ask?
again and again
Right for me and not you, that's not what we are to do
I know you can't please everybody and stay happy too
Yet
I beg to differ
The God thing is the right thing for everybody
Like it or not Jesus will come again
And
Then
After all the analyzing, wondering and movements
Who changed what, and for who
Will we all make it through
To that better world, we are now supposed to be living and striding for
Not just more for me yet for We
Kingdom work is what we must do
Now that is a "Me Too" everyone can fight for
Everyone is included

And
Forgiven of all their sins that repented for
Ideals, people, places or things
Have no order
Because this place is in order
Lead by the Highest authority
We will have no need for Democracy
When following the one who wants the best for all
We will all be included exclusively to Thee
In one body, in Christ
Oh, what a movement that will be
A World Movement that's my vision
To see everyone fulfill God's plan as he designed it in
1 Peter 4:8: "Above all, love each other deeply, because love covers over a multitude of sins."
John 15:12: "My command is this: Love each other as I have loved you."
1 Corinthians 13:13: "And now these three remain: faith, hope, and love. But the greatest of these is love."
Have we? Do we? Will we? these are the real questions that no one seems to be asking!

Notes

Notes

Notes

Notes

> If the plan is to do *Nothing*, nothing will get done, So, what's the *Plan*?
> – Carolyn Lewis

REAL

Real people
Who are they
Where are they
And
Where do they live
Real people, average, everyday folks
Are they the you or me
Are they rich or poor
We know they are not the middle class
The middle class does not exist anymore
The working poor won that war
The average person working from one paycheck to the end of the next
The everyday folks borrowing from one another, lending a hand when we can
The real people who struggle to make ends meet
Meeting only, the barest of needs
That is if you only work one job because a few is what it takes to reach what's due
Not seeing hope anywhere, close to being at hand, for you   (cont.)

Vote you say!
Then you will win!
Win what, I ask
Again and again and again
If you can relate
It is not too late
Liberty is worth fighting for
Demanding to not just be heard
Yet
Having a deciding word
Having a final say, in what affects you day by day
You have the right to not just be heard
Yet
Listened to
Afforded a seat at the table
And
Not just to eat
Yet
To make a decision to put an end to this division and fighting from within
This is what the Real People go through
Are you a Real person
Or
Just a person making it through

NOTES

Notes

Notes

NOTES

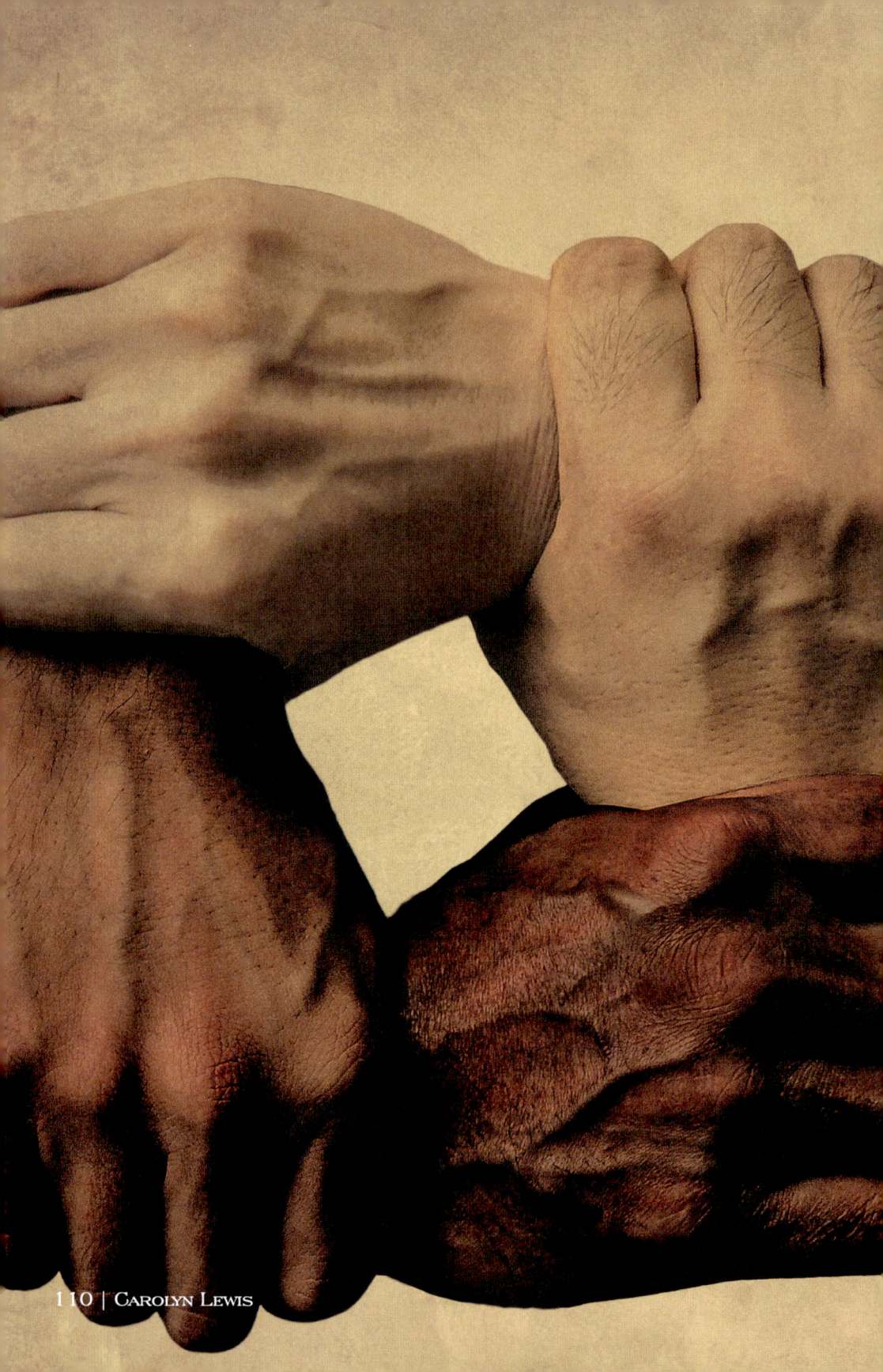

Along the Way

Along the way
Somewhere along the way we as Humans lost our way
We have forgotten what it is to pray
We have forgotten the golden rule
And
Have decided it's just easier to be
Cruel and rude
No compassion for human rights
It's just easier to fight
No
Let's not walk away
And
Pray that tomorrow will be a better day
Let's tell people off
And
Cuss people out
Because without a doubt

(cont.)

We can't be seen as being left out
Left out of the shame that others have claimed
As being what brings fame
Without a doubt, we seem to have to let the mean out
Facebook, Twitter, Instagram, Snapchat
Viral is all we want to be
At any cost
We are willing to lose
All our dignity
That is
Whatever's left after we scream and holler
For that almighty dollar
To be able to control
Our own destiny
Only to find they were all lying
There's nothing easy when it comes to
Keeping the means
Some even work harder to keep the dollar
That they believe is
The only way to true destiny
It's not easy to keep the means

As your status goes up
So do your bills
And
Your acquired needs
The tax breaks you
Once so-called hated
Are now with much appeal
Don't get so lost in what the world says matters
And
Learn to be healed
Healed from hate
And
We must tolerate
Tolerate not what Jesus came to heal
Jesus' death was not in vain
And
Who are we to say that what Jesus died for then
Is now ok
For us
To live within

Notes

Notes

Notes

Notes

The American Dream: I have found it only has two stable and consistent un-changing components.

It takes place in America and it's a dream. All other aspects and views will vary based on person, places, and ideals. There is no real model or set example.

So the real question is what are you searching for? You can no longer aspire to an ever-moving goal with no boundaries that are subject to no perspective role, define what your dream as an American should be.

THE AMERICAN DREAM HAS NO DEFINITION NOR CAN IT BE AMERICAN, IF IT IS SUBJECTED TO A DEFINITION, DESCRIBED BY A FEW TO BE DEFINED BY MILLIONS. WHAT ONCE WAS IS NO MORE ONLY BECAUSE IT NEVER REALLY EXISTED YET WAS DREAMED. SO WHAT DOES YOUR AMERICAN DREAM CONSIST OF?

DONATE TO THE SOLUTION, NOT BECAUSE OF THE CAUSE...

Here are organizations that are creating answers to America's problems. They are being proactive to issues of foreseen problems that Americans are facing daily. Please support these 501-C tax-deductible organizations by donating! Let the belief that we can and are better be the reason for donating to these worthy solutions. Not out of pity! Prayers change things. Yet prayer, support and means will create a new beginning.

Growing in Christ (TIBS) Teen Interactive Bible Study
https://growinchrist33.wixsite.com/growinginchrist

Faith Walk Ministries
https://www.faithwalkacademy.org/giving

Women's Ministries
https://www.cwmhope.org/donate-now/

Laura & George Miller Help Center of Mexico
https://www.facebook.com/The-Help-Center-217312725058364/

Mexico Sustainability Project
https://mexico-chamber.org/

Central Missouri Community Action
www.cmca.us

Let's work together for a permanent solution to an ever-growing problem, the answer lies in all of us, not just a few. We have to work for a bigger purpose than just ourselves. Cheerful giving should not be a seasonal event, but a lifetime journey of giving and receiving. Now that is a season everyone can celebrate year-round!

Made in the USA
San Bernardino, CA
01 March 2020

65177140R00071